URSULA K. LE GUIN

CONVERSATIONS ON WRITING

Published by Tin House Books, Portland, Oregon, and Brooklyn, New York

Distributed by W. W. Norton & Company

Names: Le Guin, Ursula K., 1929-2018 author, interviewee. | Naimon, David, author, interviewer.
Title: Ursula K. Le Guin : conversations on writing / [Ursula K. Le Guin] with David Naimon.
Description: First U.S. edition. | Portland, OR : Tin House Books, 2018.
Identifiers: LCCN 2018003429 | ISBN 9781941040997 (hardcover)
Subjects: LCSH: Le Guin, Ursula K., 1929—Interviews. | Le Guin, Ursula K., 1929—Authorship. | Women authors, American—20th century—Biography. | Authors, American—20th century—Interviews. | Science fiction—Authorship. | Fantasy fiction—Authorship. | Authorship. | Literature. | United States—Civilization. Classification: LCC PS3562.E42 Z46 2018 | DDC 813/.54 [B]—dc23
LC record available at https://lccn.loc.gov/2018003429

First US Edition 2018
Printed in the USA
Interior design by Jakob Vala

www.tinhouse.com

URSULA K. LE GUIN

CONVERSATIONS ON WRITING

with DAVID NAIMON

 TIN HOUSE BOOKS / Portland, Oregon & Brooklyn, New York

. . .

The copyeditor used a red pen. Ursula a pencil. Pencil and pen had agreed and disagreed on this manuscript, which Ursula had handed over just a week before. We'd emailed about blurbs just days before. Everything seemed as it should. It was now my turn to chime in where Ursula and the copyeditor disagreed. I was in the midst of doing just that when I learned she'd passed away.

More than a week has gone by and I still haven't been able to do my part. I read tributes to her by the greats—Gaiman, Atwood, Walton—finding myself without words.

I look again at Ursula's—her enthusiastic *yes!*, her matter-of-fact *I disagree.* In these gestures I see how fully present she is, how completely she attends to the task at hand, and I realize that nothing is too small to contain the whole world, to bring forth Ursula's powerful, opinionated, captivating self. The same Ursula who took on Google and Amazon on behalf of writers, who took on a boy's club in science fiction and fantasy, who now insisted the word *Earth*—the planet, our planet—should begin with a capitalized "E."

She attended to the big and small in the same way, as part of the same fabric. Realizing this, I've tried to do the same, ministering to language as she herself would've done. I'm still grieving the dream of launching this book with Ursula, us together blessing its journey. I would've been grateful to partake in any project of hers, but I'm particularly honored to be a part of this one, one of the last of her long, remarkable life.

Among the many things that made Ursula stand out as a writer, was how she imagined we could live a better future. It's up to us now, to imagine the world we want, to create the language that reflects it, to honor Ursula by honoring the Earth she has attended to so well.

—David Naimon
February 1, 2018

CONTENTS

Ursula K. Le Guin

INTRODUCTION
Fear and Loathing
in the Interview

The interviewers I fear most are the ones who've read what the publisher's PR people say about your book, along with some handy pull quotes. They read one of these aloud and say in a sincere voice, "Now, tell us more about what you said here."

Such interviewers get on well with celebrities who have written a book. It doesn't matter if the celebrity didn't actually write the book, since the interviewer hasn't actually read it. All that's wanted is a sound bite.

"Tell us more about this" may also work with serious authors whose book contains information or a message they're eager to repeat in order to make sure it gets delivered.

But it fails with authors who have worked hard to put something complicated into words as well as they possibly can. They're happy to hear what they said read aloud, but not happy with the implication that it needs to be said differently or better. "What you wrote about the nightingale is so interesting, Mr. Keats, please tell us more?"

I've been fortunate enough to meet the polar opposite of this uninformed interviewer. A couple of sessions with Bill Moyers set my permanent standard of The Good Interview. It's the one you wish could go on. It's a *conversation* between people who have thought about what they're talking about, and are thinking about it now in the light of what the other person is saying. This leads each of them to say things that they may be just discovering. They may not agree, may even have quite fundamental disagreements, but such differences, spoken and answered without belligerence, can take the conversation to a high level of intensity and honesty.

By now I know within a question or two whether we're heading for frustration or reward. If the signs of doom are clear, going on with it is hard work for both of us. I think, "How am I supposed to answer *that*?" while the interviewer thinks, "Oh god, another ten seconds of silence and then she says, *Um.*"

The good interview is like a good badminton rally: you know right away that the two of you can keep that birdie in the air, and all you have to do is watch it fly.

Facing each other for the first time in one of KBOO's lovable, terminally funky recording rooms, David and I were a bit stiff and shy, but we soon got going, and I knew our bird was on the wing.

As a novelist I can talk and do talk shamelessly about fiction, but am shy and amateurish speaking as a poet. People who talk about poetry are usually talking to other poets, and Other Poets are a demanding, fiercely opinionated, often adversarial lot. They can be clannish, too. On performance nights at writing workshops, I've sat with prose writers listening intently as the poets read; when it was the prose writers' turn to read, the poets all got up and left. And then there's a kind of Poetspeak that goes with the territory, but which is not my language. All in all, I was nervous about the poetry interview with David. But that lasted no time. Nothing cures nervousness quicker than getting interested in the conversation.

Having to talk about my nonfiction scares me in a different way. I fear the interviewer is going to discuss the influence on my work of Schopenhauer, or Wittgenstein, or Theodor Adorno, none of whom I have ever read; or will demand my opinion of queer theory, or string theory; or instruct me to tell the audience what Taoism is; or (likeliest of all) will ask me about The Future of Mankind. That I know the immensity of my ignorance doesn't mean I like to *display* it. I'm grateful to an interviewer who respects the limits of my learning and my intellect, and who doesn't require me to act the Oracle of Delphi.

And every now and then I meet one who realizes that what I really like to do is *talk shop*.

David likes talking shop too. So that's what we did.

I want to thank KBOO for letting us do it. And for being for fifty years the strongest consistent voice in Oregon of and for the arts and the freedom and generosity of thought. While America is busy tearing itself apart into factions with rant, lies, and mindless violence, it's in voices like this that you can hear—if you listen—what may yet hold us together.

—Ursula K. Le Guin,
October 6, 2017

ON FICTION

"Children know perfectly well that unicorns aren't real," says Ursula K. Le Guin. "But they also know that books about unicorns, if they are good books, are true books."

That was my experience of reading *Tales of Earthsea* growing up. Magic is commonplace in Earthsea. Wizards walk the earth and dragons fly the skies. Yet the further they took me from "reality" the closer I felt to the real. Ursula K. Le Guin at her heart is a writer not of fiction per se, but of the imagination. And imagination, to her, is not something we merely do in our spare moments, an idle act, but the very faculty that makes us who we are. So much so that she warns us that "people who deny the existence of dragons are often eaten by dragons. From within."

Having been transported on the wings of Le Guin's imaginative powers from a young age, I couldn't help but wonder what meeting the "real" Ursula K. Le Guin would be like, how the imagined writer, a wizard who conjured worlds—the magic realm of the *Tales of Earthsea*, the ambisexual planet of Gethen in *The Left Hand of Darkness*, the anarcho-syndicalist society of Anarres in *The Dispossessed*, to name just a few—would compare to the real-world, flesh-and-blood woman in Portland, Oregon, the one who walked the same everyday streets as me, the one I would soon interview about the nuts and bolts craft of writing fiction.

We met at the studios of KBOO, a largely volunteer-run community radio station in Portland's inner eastside, to have this conversation, and my first impression of Ursula there was one of matter-of-fact groundedness. Of someone who didn't suffer fools. Someone whose wealth of experience had not merely accumulated over a long life well-lived, but had become something else altogether, had alchemized into a sort of lived-in wisdom. And with this wisdom there seemed to be no patience for masks, for pretense. Confirmed again and again as we talked, my first impression of her became my lasting one.

Was there a contradiction between this real, of-this-world Ursula and the imagined otherwordly one? Strangely, there didn't seem to be. The real and the imagined were inseparable, a well-rooted writer whose imagination branched high into the sky. Yet, the more I learned about Ursula's way in the world outside her books, the more it seemed as if it were the unseen, the imaginary within them, that was animating the real, not the other way around.

Despite her stature in the world at large—named a "Grandmaster of Science Fiction" by the Science Fiction & Fantasy Writers of America, and a "Living Legend" by the Library of Congress—she continues to publish with small independent presses, from the anarchist PM Press in Oakland to the feminist science fiction publisher Aqueduct Press in Seattle, as well as appear on stations like KBOO that share with her a certain communitarian ethos and a concern for amplifying the voices of the marginalized and under-represented. I can't help but suspect that the imagined worlds of Earthsea, of Gethen, of Anarres, these imagined alternative ways of being, in relation to each other and to the land, are the true, if invisible, animators of these real-world gestures of hers.

And I was soon to discover that even the seemingly most mundane of things—grammar, syntax, sentence structure—even these are animated by something unseen, dare I say, magical, behind and beyond them. That the length of our sentences, their gait, their sound, that our use of tense, of point of view, of pronouns, all have their histories, their stories, their political and cultural implications, and each could be a building block, a concrete gesture, for good or for ill, toward an imagined future world.

—David Naimon

• • •

DAVID NAIMON: In most art forms—painting, dancing, music—it seems like imitation is part of the learning process, that it is crucial to honing one's craft and finding one's voice. Even the most experimental and innovative painter usually has a period of painting like their predecessors. You don't shy away from recommending imitation as a way to learn to write but it seems like it is something that writers have traditionally been a little troubled by.

URSULA K. LE GUIN: Maybe not traditionally, but more recently, yes. In the arts, imitation has to be understood by the person doing it as a learning device; otherwise it's plagiarism. You imitate only to learn, and you don't publish it. Or if you do, you say, "This is an imitation of Hemingway." But the internet, and competition in college, tends to blur the distinction between imitation and plagiarism, and this blurriness leads teachers to warn people not to imitate—and that's foolish. You have to learn by reading good stuff and trying to write that way. If a piano player never heard any other piano player, how would he know what to do? We're not using imitation as it could be used, I think.

DN: You've often talked about the importance of sound, that the sound of language is where it all begins, and that language is, at its core, a physical thing.

UKL: I hear what I write. I started writing poetry when I was really young. I always heard it in my head. I realized that a lot of people who write about writing don't seem to hear it, don't listen to it, their perception is more theoretical and intellectual. But if it's happening in your body, if you are hearing what you write, then you can listen for the right cadence, which will help the sentence run clear. And what young writers always talk about—"finding your voice"—well, you can't find your own voice if you aren't listening for it. The sound of your writing is an essential part of what it's doing. Our teaching of writing tends to ignore it, except maybe in poetry. And so we get prose that goes *clunk, clunk, clunk*. And we don't know what's wrong with it.

DN: You have this wonderful quote from your talk at Portland Arts & Lectures in 2000:

> Beneath memory and experience, beneath imagination and invention, beneath words, there are rhythms to which memory and imagination and words all move. The writer's job is to go down deep enough to feel that rhythm, find it, move to it, be moved by it, and let it move memory and imagination to find words.

UKL: That is something that I learned from Virginia Woolf, who talks about it most wonderfully in a letter to her friend Vita. Style, she says, is rhythm—the "wave in the mind"—the wave, the rhythm are there before the words, and bring the words to fit it.

DN: You've cited Woolf as perhaps the best example of the use of rhythm.

UKL: She's an amazing example of the use of a long and subtle rhythm in prose. But there are many, many others. I wrote an essay about the rhythm of Tolkien's writing in *The Lord of the Rings.* Short rhythms repeated form long rhythms; there's a cyclical repetition in his work which I think is part of why it totally enchants so many of us. We are caught in this rhythm and are happy there.

DN: It's interesting how you emphasize the importance of understanding grammar and grammar terminology but also the importance of interrogating its rules. You point out that it is a strange phenomenon that grammar is the tool of our trade and yet so many writers steer away from an engagement with it.

FROM
Virginia Woolf's
To the Lighthouse

. . .

Then indeed peace had come. Messages of peace breathed from the sea to the shore. Never to break its sleep any more, to lull it rather more deeply to rest, and whatever the dreamers dreamt holily, dreamt wisely, to confirm—what else was it murmuring—as Lily Briscoe laid her head on the pillow in the clean still room and heard the sea. Through the open window the voice of the beauty of the world came murmuring, too softly to hear exactly what it said—but what mattered if the meaning were plain?

FROM
J. R. R. Tolkien's
The Fellowship of the Ring

. . .

Upon great pedestals founded in the deep waters stood two great kings of stone: still with blurred eyes and crannied brows they frowned upon the North. The left hand of each was raised palm outwards in gesture of warning; in each right hand there was an axe; upon each head there was a crumbling helm and crown. Great power and majesty they still wore, the silent wardens of a long-vanished kingdom.

UKL: In my generation and for a while after—I was born in 1929—we were taught grammar right from the start. It was quietly drilled into us. We knew the names of the parts of speech, we had a working acquaintance with how English works, which they don't get in most schools anymore. There is so much less reading in schools, and very little teaching of grammar. For a writer this is kind of like being thrown into a carpenter's shop without ever having learned the names of the tools or handled them consciously. What do you do with a Phillips screwdriver? What *is* a Phillips screwdriver? We're not equipping people to write; we're just saying, "You too can write!" or "Anybody can write, just sit down and do it!" But to make anything, you've got to have the tools to make it.

DN: You talk about the usefulness of diagramming sentences, that by diagramming them you discover that sentences have skeletons.

UKL: I wasn't taught that in school—that was the previous generation. My mother and my great-aunt could diagram a sentence, and they showed me how. I enjoyed it; for anyone who has that kind of mind, it's illuminating. It's kind of like drawing the skeleton of a horse. You go: "Oh, that's how they hang together!"

DN: It's interesting to think that if sentences have skeletons then different sentences are, in a sense, different animals. This would bring us back to rhythm, as they would all have a different rhythm, a different sound, because they would walk differently.

UKL: A different gait, right. Although all the sentences in a piece would also be following a certain underlying, integrating rhythm.

DN: Every so often in your book on writing, *Steering the Craft*, you have an opinion piece, and one of my favorites is about morality and grammar. You talk about how morality and language are linked, but that

George Orwell's *1984*

• • •

"It was a bright cold day in April,
and the clocks were striking thirteen."

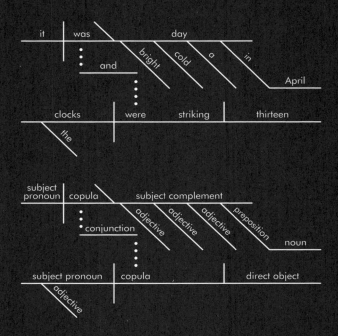

morality and correctness are not the same thing. Yet we often confuse them in the realm of grammar.

UKL: The "grammar bullies"—you read them in places like the *New York Times,* and they tell you what is correct: *You must never use "hopefully." "Hopefully, we will be going there on Tuesday." That is incorrect and wrong and you are basically an ignorant pig if you say it.* This is judgmentalism. The game that is being played there is a game of social class. It has nothing to do with the morality of writing and speaking and thinking clearly, which Orwell, for instance, talked about so well. It's just affirming that I am from a higher class than you are. The trouble is that people who aren't taught grammar very well in school fall for these statements from these pundits, delivered with vast authority from above. I'm fighting that. A very interesting case in point is using "they" as a singular. This offends the grammar bullies endlessly; it is wrong, wrong, wrong! Well, it was right until the eighteenth century, when they invented the rule that "he" includes "she."

It didn't exist in English before then; Shakespeare used "they" instead of "he or she"—we all do, we always have done, in speaking, in colloquial English. It took the women's movement to bring it back to English literature. And it is important. Because it's a crossroads between correctness bullying and the moral use of language. If "he" includes "she" but "she" doesn't include "he," a big statement is being made, with huge social and moral implications. But we don't have to use "he" that way—we've got "they." Why not use it?

DN: This difference between grammatical correctness and the ways language engages moral questions reminds me of this quote of yours: "We can't restructure society without restructuring the English language." That the battle is essentially as much at the sentence level as it is in the world.

UKL: As a freshman in college I read George Orwell's great essay about how writing English clearly is a political matter. It went really deep into me. Often I'm simply rephrasing Orwell.

DN: It's reflected in your work as well. I think of *The Dispossessed*, your novel about an anarchist utopia. There is no property in this imagined world and there are also no possessive pronouns. The world and the language of the world are reflecting back upon each other.

UKL: The founders of this anarchist society made up a new language because they realized you couldn't have a new society and an old language. They based the new language on the old one but changed it enormously. It's simply an illustration of what Orwell was saying.

DN: Lots of these rules of grammatical correctness that reflect some regressive tendencies in society, you call "fake rules." In *Steering the Craft*, you talk about the importance of engaging with our tools, understanding the power of punctuation and understanding grammar, but also warn us to be careful not to fall for these fake rules. One of them is the generic pronoun "he" to refer to both men and women, what amounts to an erasure of women at the sentence level. Is it true that you've said that if you could rewrite *Left Hand of Darkness*, a book, way ahead of its time, about gender fluidity, you would make some changes like this on the sentence level?

UKL: Obviously it is unsatisfactory to call these genderless people "he" throughout the book, as I do (unless one of them goes into "kemmer" and gains gender, becomes genuinely if temporarily "he" or "she"). In 1968, "they" was simply not an option; no editor would have published the book. Soon after the book was written several novels came out using made-up pronouns to blur gender, but I couldn't do it; I can't do that to English. So what to do? I rewrote a chapter of *Left Hand of Darkness* making everybody "she" instead of "he," and it is interesting to read it after having read

. . .

There was a wall. It did not look important. It was built of uncut rocks roughly mortared. An adult could look right over it, and even a child could climb it. Where it crossed the roadway, instead of having a gate it degenerated into mere geometry, a line, an idea of boundary. But the idea was real. It was important. For seven generations there had been nothing in the world more important than that wall.

Like all walls it was ambiguous, two-faced. What was inside it and what was outside it depended upon which side of it you were on.

. . .

And I saw then again, and for good, what I had always been afraid to see, and had pretended not to see in him: that he was a woman as well as a man. Any need to explain the sources of that fear vanished with the fear; what I was left with was, at last, acceptance of him as he was. Until then I had rejected him, refused him his own reality. He had been quite right to say that he, the only person on Gethen who trusted me, was the only Gethenian I distrusted. For he was the only one who had entirely accepted me as a human being: who had liked me personally and given me entire personal loyalty, and who therefore had demanded of me an equal degree of recognition, of acceptance. I had not been willing to give it. I had been afraid to give it. I had not wanted to give my trust, my friendship to a man who was a woman, a woman who was a man.

the "he" version. But it's not right either. They aren't "she." They're "they." And we can't use "it." I envy the Finnish, and I think the Japanese at least in some respects, that they can speak genderlessly.

DN: Just as you've pointed out the erasure of women at the sentence level you've also voiced concerns about the ways in which women writers get disappeared from the conversation, particularly when it comes to entering or not entering the canon. I think in one conversation someone asked you for examples and you mentioned Grace Paley as someone sliding out of the conversation.

UKL: I fear for Grace's reputation, because it happens so often that a woman writer, very much admired but not best-seller famous, however admired by many critics, just slides out of sight after her death . . . and the place is filled by a man. Well, no man could possibly fill Grace Paley's place. She wrote extraordinarily as a woman. And that may be part of the problem.

DN: When I interviewed Jo Walton we engaged this question as well. She said it is often difficult in any given moment or instance to know whether sexism is happening but if you step back and look at the way the canon is being formed—in this case we were talking about the canon in science fiction and fantasy—it becomes clearer. She brought up the example of William Gibson. *Neuromancer* won the Hugo and many other awards and around the same time C. J. Cherryh also won the Hugo and seemed to be informing the conversation at large, like Gibson. She went on to win the Hugo again six or seven years later, and seemed to be just as successful. But now, years later you look back and Gibson is in the canon and there are a lot of people who have never even heard of C. J. Cherryh.

UKL: That's true. Why hasn't she been reprinted? Why isn't she talked about? There's something slightly mysterious about this. What is misogyny? A male need to establish a male world? But it is a mystery—I can't take it any further.

DN: You've been an outspoken critic of the increasing commodification of authors and how sales departments are taking over from editorial. That a lot of the choices that influence how a book is being shaped are less about art and more about commerce. You've pushed back against this, and argued that literature shouldn't just be viewed in terms of what's in vogue. It doesn't seem like you're *against* what is in vogue, but you've tried to expand the conversation beyond popular contemporary choices in stories and novels, like present tense and very short sentences.

UKL: There are advantages and disadvantages to living a very long time, as I have. One of the advantages is that you can't help having a long view. You've seen it come and seen it go. Something that's being announced as the absolute only way to write, you recognize as a fashion, a fad, trendy—the way to write *right now* if you want to sell *right now* to a *right now* editor. But there's also the long run to consider. Nothing's deader than last year's trend.

DN: Can you discuss the cost/benefit trade-off when choosing past or present tense? You've talked before about how past tense allows for more ready movement back and forth in time, that it more closely mimics the ways our minds and memories work.

UKL: And it is particularly connected to telling a big story, a story with some real depth. But it is a complicated issue. Obviously the present tense has certain uses that it's wonderfully suited for. But recently it has been adopted blindly, as the only way to tell a story—often by young writers who haven't read very much. Well, it's a good way to tell some stories, not a good way to tell others. It's inherently limiting. I call it "flashlight focus." You see a spot ahead of you and it is dark all around it. That's great for high suspense, high drama, cut-to-the-chase writing. But if you want to tell a big, long story, like the books of Elena Ferrante, or Jane Smiley's *The Last Hundred Years* trilogy, which moves year by year from 1920 to 2020—the present tense would cripple those books. To assume that the present tense is literally "now" and the past tense literally remote in time is extremely naïve.

DN: I would definitely encourage writers to look at your book reviews to see your thoughts on craft in context, in direct engagement with a specific piece of art. For instance, in your review of David Mitchell's *The Bone Clocks* for the *Guardian* you discuss this issue of present tense. It's a great review. You compare Virginia Woolf's stream of consciousness to what you call Mitchell's "stream of self-consciousness." And you also bring up some of these issues around time. Here is what you said:

> Here, in a novel deeply concerned with Time, there is virtually no past tense. Present-tense narration is now taken for granted by many fiction readers because everything they read, from internet news to texting, is in the present tense, but at this great length it can be hard going. Past-tense narration easily implies previous

times and extends into the misty reaches of the subjunctive, the conditional, the future; but the pretense of a continuous eyewitness account admits little relativity of times, little connection between events. The present tense is a narrowbeam flashlight in the dark, limiting the view to the next step—now, now, now. No past, no future. The world of the infant, of the animal, perhaps of the immortal.

That seems so wonderfully put.

UKL: Good. [Laughs.] David Mitchell is a writer worth writing about.

DN: Let's talk about point of view. The choice of first-person point of view is more popular today than ever. You've talked about how first person was mainly found in medieval diaries and saints' confessions and then in Montaigne's essays, and was not a big part of our literature until recently.

UKL: Third-person limited is very similar to first person in that it is one point of view only. One or the other of those two do seem to be, over and over, the only point of view used in contemporary fiction.

DN: But it is actually pretty late in the history of literature that both these points of view arise.

UKL: Henry James did the limited third person really well, showing us the way to do it. He milked that cow successfully. And it's a great cow, it still gives lots of milk. But if you read only contemporary stuff, always third-person limited, you don't realize that point of view in a story is very important and can be very movable. It's here where I suggest that people read books like Woolf's *To the Lighthouse* to see what she does by moving from mind to mind. Or Tolstoy's *War and Peace* for goodness' sake. Wow. The way he slides from one point of view to another without you knowing that you've changed point of view—he does it so gracefully. You know where you are, whose eyes you are seeing through, but you don't have the sense of being jerked from place to place. That's mastery of a craft.

DN: And you put forth that the omniscient point of view is a legitimate choice for contemporary writing.

UKL: Any of us who grew up reading eighteenth- or nineteenth-century fiction are perfectly at home with what is called "omniscience." I myself call it "authorial" point of view because the term "omnisicence," the idea of an author being omniscient, is so often used in a judgmental way, as if it were a bad thing. But the author after all *is* the author of all these characters, the maker, the inventor of them. In fact all the characters *are* the author if you come right down to the honest truth of it. So the author has the perfect right to know what they're thinking. If the author doesn't tell you what they are thinking . . . why? This is worth thinking about. Often it's simply to spin out suspense by not telling you what the author knows. Well, that's legitimate. This is art. But I'm trying to get people to think about their choices here, because there are so many beautiful choices that are going unused. In a way, first person and limited third are the easiest ones, the least interesting.

DN: You've mentioned that in writing workshops the most common mistake you've seen is what you call "inconsistent point of view."

UKL: That's when you shift from one person's mind to another's, the way Tolstoy and Woolf do so splendidly, but you do it awkwardly or you do it without knowing you are doing it. The thing about point of view is awareness. Changing it requires intense awareness and a certain amount of practice and skill in the shifting. Successful shifting gives binocular or more than binocular vision. Instead of a single view of an event, you do what *Rashomon* does, offer multiple perspectives, but without having to retell the story multiple times as *Rashomon* does. You can do it as you tell the story, and the multiple points of view lead to greater puzzlement or greater clarity about what is going on, depending upon what you want. I think the authorial point of view, because it allows such shifting, is the most flexible and useful of all the points of view. It's the freest.

DN: It wasn't until reading *Steering the Craft* that I realized just how experimental Charles Dickens's *Bleak House* was. You discuss it, not necessarily as a text to emulate, but to show some of the radical choices he made both in terms of how he alternates point of view and also how he alternates tense.

UKL: Half the book is written in the present tense, very unusual in that period. And those are the passages written in the authorial point of view—an almost eagle-eye view, rare at any time. It's an extraordinary book.

DN: You've said that modernist writing manuals often conflate story with conflict. What do you mean by this?

UKL: Well, to preach that story is conflict, always to ask, "Where's the conflict in your story?"—this needs some thinking about. If you say that story is about conflict, that plot must be based on conflict, you're limiting your view of the world severely. And in a sense making a political statement: that life is conflict, so in stories conflict is all that really matters. This is simply untrue. To see life as a battle is a narrow, social-Darwinist view, and a very masculine one. Conflict, of course, is part of life, I'm not saying you should try to keep it out of your stories, just that it's not their only lifeblood. Stories are about a lot of different things.

DN: It's amazing how quickly we fall into battle metaphors in common speech when speaking about almost anything.

UKL: I do try to avoid saying "the fight" for such and such, "the war" against such and such. I resist putting everything into terms of conflict and immediate violent resolution. I don't think that existence works that way. I'm trying to remember what Lao Tzu says about conflict. He limits it to the battlefield, where it belongs. To limit all human behavior to conflict is to leave out vast, rich areas of human experience.

DN: You raise this issue in your otherwise very positive review of the latest novel by Salman Rushdie. Your concern is that the dark jinni in the book, the force of destruction, is inextricably linked to the creative impulse in a way that gave you pause.

UKL: Yes. At the very end of the book there is a suggestion that if we aren't forever at war we will be peaceable and boring and dull and not do anything worth doing. All I can say is that's not my experience of war and peace. I was a kid during the Second World War. All-out war is not a period where creativity gets much play. Coming out of that war was like coming out of a very dark place into an open world where you could think and do something other than

41

war, the war effort, fighting. Where there was room for creation, not just destruction.

DN: You've been a strong voice behind the idea that science fiction and fantasy are as much literature as realist or mimetic fiction or memoir. At one time you even said, "Fake realism is the escapism of our time." You describe a long uninterrupted lineage for fantasy back to the Mahābhārata and *Beowulf.*

UKL: I was just trying to point out that possibly the oldest form of literature is fantastic. It begins in myths and legends, and in hero stories that become mythologized, like *The Odyssey.* But I think the exclusion of genre writing from literature is in the past now. It's hard for me to stop talking in those terms, though, because I had to keep arguing for so long that genre is literature just as much as *The Grapes of Wrath* is. Of course most of it isn't as good—but most realism isn't as good as *The Grapes of Wrath* either. Judgment by genre is just wrong—stupid, wasteful. Most people know that now.

DN: This makes me think of the essay you wrote back in 1974, "Why are Americans Afraid of Dragons?" and makes we wonder if perhaps we are starting to come to terms with dragons in America now?

UKL: Yes and no. That's a wider thing than the genre/literature argument. A fear of using the imagination is very deep in America. It shows in our schools, where apparently kids read less and less and less fiction. And do they get any poetry at all anymore? How does our education train and exercise the imagination? Well, I don't know, so I shouldn't talk about it.

DN: *Steering the Craft* engages this conversation and complicates it in a good way, I think. In the book you omnivorously quote from Virginia Woolf and Mark Twain and Charles Dickens but also from Margaret Atwood and J. R. R. Tolkien and even from Native tales, like the story of the Thunder Badger, as examples of different techniques. You fluidly move between these worlds, which you can also see in your own fiction, these varied influences. But it feels in a way that you are making a quiet statement in the craft book that these are all literatures.

UKL: Absolutely. In a recent online workshop in narrative fiction at Book View Café, I found that over and over again I want to send people to read Patrick O'Brian's sea stories, for his long sentences, or for his descriptions. If you want to see how to write a sea battle, go to O'Brian. He is an incredibly good action writer. But how does he do it? He's certainly worth studying. Within genre you can find marvelous examples of writing.

DN: You have been very interested in Taoism and Buddhism over the years and translated your own version of the *Tao Te Ching*. How do you see that influencing your writing? Are you able to articulate a way in which you feel those are influencing story?

UKL: It goes so deep that it is hard for me to articulate. I'm not good at analyzing my own writing.

The Lathe of Heaven is an obvious example of using a Taoist approach to life. Though I didn't use the I Ching to write the book, the way Philip K. Dick did to write *The Man in the High Castle*, the movement is continuous change, and in *Lathe* it happens through dreams. So you never quite know if it is a dream or if it is real. That is my book where the Asian influence is most clearly on the surface. But that sense that everything is always moving and changing—well, if you ask me what story is about, it's about change.

DN: I may be reading too much into this quote of yours, but this felt like it evoked something about Buddhist philosophy with regard to the relationship of self to art. You say: "Some people see art as a matter of control. I see it mostly as a matter of self-control. It's like this, in me there's a story that wants to be told. It is my end. I am its means. If I can keep myself, my ego, my wishes and opinions, my mental junk, out of the way, and find the focus of the story, and follow the movement of the story, the story will tell itself . . ."

This feels like a very different approach to story than one of willfulness to put something down on the page.

UKL: Yes, that's fairly Taoistic. That is *wu wei*, or doing by not doing. It seems very passive. Of course, Lao Tzu strikes the Western conflict-oriented mind as incredibly passive. "Don't do something, just sit there." That's where he is so tricky and so useful. There are many different ways of just sitting there.

DN: In *Steering the Craft*, you include exercises with each chapter. Do you have a favorite? Or one that writers find particularly useful/challenging?

UKL: As I say in the book, "Chastity" was one I invented when I was fourteen, when I realized that my attempts to write stories weren't exactly flowery, but had too many words, too many adjectives and adverbs. So I deliberately tried to write a whole page of narrative without any adjectives or adverbs at all. It gets very tough, because essential words like "only" and "then" are adverbial. So sometimes you can't cut them all out. But you can certainly cut out all the "-ly" words, and all the rich juicy adjectives. You end up with a chaste, plain piece of prose. And because you have to put all that energy into the verbs and the nouns instead, it is stronger and richer. "Chastity" is an exercise I've used in almost every workshop I've ever taught. And people hate it! But they don't hate it as bad as the last exercise, "A Terrible Thing to Do," where you take a piece of your own writing and cut it in half, saying the same things in half as many words.

DN: You mentioned that you recently started an on-line engagement with aspiring writers. I wonder if your own personal biography might also be a source of inspiration for people trying to find their feet as writers. It took you quite a while, of writing and submitting, before you saw any tangible success. Can you talk about that period, how long it was, what you were doing, etc.?

UKL: In doing this workshop it seems to be useful for me, now at the end of my career, to tell people some of what I went through. It feels sort of egoistic, but it may be of some real interest and value to them to know of the setbacks and awful self-doubts that I think most writers go through. More than most artists, maybe because they work so much in solitude, writers tend to self-doubt. And getting published is a formidable barrier. Starting out, I was able to place a poem every now and then—in one of the little tiny poetry magazines—eight or nine readers—but at least I was in print. But I couldn't sell any fiction. For six or seven years I was methodically writing short stories and novels, trying to place them, and getting nowhere. Got lots of nice rejection slips.

The fact is, I was committed to being a writer, to my writing, and I had a self-confidence or arrogance that carried me through. "I am going to do it, and I'm going to do it my way." I stuck to that. And bang, I finally broke through. I sold two stories in one week, one to a commercial magazine and one to a little literary magazine. Once the door cracks open, it seems to stay open. It's easier to know where to submit your work. My stories often weren't conventionally realistic, but had some nonrealistic twist, and I realized that fantasy and science fiction magazines could read them and not say, "What *is* this?" There was an open mind there that I hadn't met in the conventional markets. After this breakthrough, slowly but fairly steadily, I began to get the breaks.

Of course, until I had an agent, I faithfully submitted my work, which is hard work.

And this is the area I'm not sure I know how to talk about now—it's so different, with the internet, e-publication, self-publication. About self-publication, for instance, I can't even say I'm of two minds. I'm just trying to figure out what it really involves and where it really gets you as a writer. If you self-publish without any network of publicity, any way to make your work known, and if you don't choose to sell yourself to advertisers—? I just don't know. I don't know. It's wonderful to see your work in print, goodness knows, but how much good is that if nobody's reading it outside your peer group and your relatives? I don't know. Nobody has much solid advice to give anybody at this point. We're in a revolution. We can only try to figure out how publishing is going to settle down after the revolution. And it will.

ON POETRY

Prior to my first interview with Ursula, my wife and I were planning a hiking trip to the North Cascades National Park along the border between Washington State and Canada. But wildfires, the new summer norm in the Pacific Northwest, had another idea, shutting down the park and sending us scrambling for last-minute alternatives. I knew of Ursula's long-standing love of Steens Mountain in the remote high desert of the farthest corner of southeastern Oregon, a landscape that had informed the world of her novel *The Tombs of Atuan*, as well as her poetry-photography collaborative collection *Out Here*. Even though we had yet to meet, I decided to call her up and see if, by chance, she had any suggestions to save our vacation.

"Do you know about dark skies?" Ursula asked, clearly excited to share. "That this is one of the only places left in the United States where you can experience true darkness, see the stars as if under a sky with virtually no light pollution?" she continued, her voice full of the wonder of countless nights under that very sky.

Soon my wife and I found ourselves "out there," in a town of fewer than twenty people, in a hotel run by fifth-generation Oregonians, in a region where wild horses still roamed under the brightest of dark skies. "Tell them Ursula and Charles sent you," she told us, and we were taken in and cared for by the rare breed of people who lived out there, farmers and ranchers who could trace an unbroken lineage back to the first white settlers in the region. As my wife and I sat together beneath the "blazing silence," "the endless abyss of light," contemplating our place in the world, in the universe, we were, unbeknownst to us, learning about Ursula through these dark skies and the people they illuminated, long before Ursula and I were to meet face-to-face.

Now, when I think of Ursula's poetry it's this, these unadulterated skies and the people who generation after generation have lived beneath them, I think of most. If *imagination* is the word that comes first to mind about her fiction, *contemplation* is the word I'd most associate with her poetry. She does not write science fiction poems, poems taking place in imagined other worlds, but rather contemplates our place in this one. If one removes human light from the sky, allowing it to become again "eternity made visible," if one spends time in a land where antelope, coyote, pelicans, and raptors far outnumber human souls, certain questions of meaning inevitably arise. What does true fellowship with the nonhuman other—animals, birds, plants, the land itself—look like? What human tools and technologies, stories and language, are worth passing on generation to generation? What is our proper relationship to mystery, to wonder, to what we don't know, to what we can't?

Ursula's world is not a Manichean world, one where darkness and light are in opposition. "Yin and yang" can be translated as "dark-bright" and for Ursula, much like in the precepts of Taoism, these seeming opposites are actually one thing, inseparable, interconnected, and interdependent. The people of the world of Earthsea wrote and passed down many Taoist-like poem-songs, none older than the poem of their own creation myth. This culture chose to pass down this poem, generation after generation, to contemplate "dark-brightness" and their place within it. And Ursula, fittingly, chose an excerpt from it as the epigraph to the book that introduces their world to us, a world that still strove for harmony and balance with otherness:

> Only in silence the word,
> Only in dark the light,
> Only in dying life:
> Bright the hawk's flight
> On the empty sky.

Each summer since our summer in the Steens, the wildfires have worsened and spread. The contemplation of nature is now an inevitably political thing. As we continue to look up at a sky that has been humanized, that reflects back our own light, our own selves, rather than that of otherness, that no longer prompts us to pause in awe and contemplate, the opportunities to create fellowship seem to diminish. It's the attentiveness of poetry, of Ursula's poetry in particular, that enacts ways to still do so.

—David Naimon

∙ ∙ ∙

DAVID NAIMON: You've talked about the phenom-enon that happens sometimes when you're writing a novel, that you hear a voice, the voice of another in-side of you, a voice that becomes the character that tells the story for you. I was wondering if you feel like writing poetry involves a similar voice.

URSULA K. LE GUIN: Well, that's complicated. I don't write very many persona poems, which is the equivalent of the voice of a character dictating to you in a novel. I have written some, but poems come in their own, dif-ferent way. It tends to be a few words or even just a beat, with a kind of aura about them, and you know then that there is the possibility of a poem there. Sometimes they come very easily, but I've never felt like I was taking dictation with a poem the way I have felt with novels, like the voice speaking through me was so certain of what it wanted to say that I didn't have to argue.

DN: I know you don't write haiku, but there are a lot of poems in *Late in the Day* that I suspected might share a sensibility with haiku. It drove me to Robert Hass's introduction to *The Essential Haiku* to see if my instincts were true in this regard. Hass says that haikus are attentive to time and space, that they are grounded in a season of the year, that the language is kept plain with accurate original images drawn from common life, and that there's a sense of the human place within the cyclical nature of the world. Do you recognize those qualities in your poems?

UKL: Yes, I feel totally at home with that. The thing about haiku is the form doesn't work for me in English. I don't think syllabically, I think rhythmically. The syllable count just doesn't give form to me.

That's a shortcoming in me, not in the form, so my equivalent of the haiku is the quatrain, which is, of course, a very old English form, with mostly iambic or trochaic rhythm, and often with rhyme.

DN: Are there some particular examples of poets who write in quatrains that you love?

UKL: A. E. Housman is the absolute master of the quatrain. I grew up with Housman from twelve or thirteen on. He goes deep.

DN: *Booklist* has a review of one of your earlier collections called *Going Out with Peacocks*, and in it, the reviewer says that the book can be divided into poems about nature from which political concerns are not entirely absent, and other poems that are political where nature is not entirely absent. [Le Guin laughs.] This seems true of the poems of *Late in the Day* as well. It's interesting how, even in the nature poems we get the sense, in the background, of either political concern or political uneasiness. You frame this well in the foreword to the collection, a reprint of a talk you gave at the "Anthropocene: Arts of Living on a Damaged Planet" conference at UC Santa Cruz.

UKL: How can you write about nature now without—well, I guess we have to call it politics—but without what we have done to our world getting into the poem? It's pretty hard to leave that out entirely.

DN: But if a reader were to skip the foreword and read some of the poems, one might think, on first glance, that there is nothing political in *Late in the Day*. The foreword seems to suggest that the advocacy for stillness and silence and fellowship is, in and of itself, a radical act.

UKL: Yeah, I suppose so. Yes.

DN: There are many nods in this collection to the relationship to time.

Riding the Coast Starlight

I saw white pelicans rise
from the waters of morning
in the wide valley, going.
I saw trees white with snow
rise silent from clouds
in the deep mountains, returning.
Heavy, noble, solemn the gesture
of the wings, the branches, a white writing destruction.

UKL: It is, after all, called *Late in the Day.* [Laughs.] It was written in my mid-eighties, so there's a lot about that.

DN: At various moments you say, "Time is being," "Time is the temple," and in "The Canada Lynx" you evoke the virtue of moving in silence through space without a track and disappearing. This sentiment feels very much akin to Taoism, to a Taoist evocation of time and space.

UKL: There is almost certainly Taoism in it, because it got so deep in me and everything I do. There's some Buddhism, too, and of course "The Canada Lynx" is also an elegy, because we're losing the lynxes—they are leaving quietly. So, there's a mixed feeling there— it's praise for being able to move quietly but also lament for the disappearance, for the going away.

DN: In the foreword you talk about the importance of fellowship with the nonhuman other. And by "nonhuman other" you are referring not just to animals and plants, but also stones and even the objects that we as humans have fashioned for our own use. Your poem "The Small Indian Pestle at the Applegate House" is a great example of this. The repetition of words—hand, held, hold—really evokes this sense of repeated fellowship, not only with the object but also with others who have used it before and with the person who originally made it. In that same speech you talk about being against the idea of the "techno-fix." I bet a lot of people assume when they see this, a poem about a pestle, and a philosophy opposed to the techno-fix, that you are antitechnology.

UKL: Oh, yeah. I'm labeled a Luddite instantly.

DN: Can you parse that out a little bit for us? Because it seems like the pestle is a technology just as language is a technology.

UKL: Of course it is, it's a great technology, and it lasted us for hundreds of thousands of years. My objection

. . .

The Small Indian Pestle at
the Applegate House

Dense, heavy, fine-grained, dark basalt
worn river-smooth all round, a cylinder
with blunt round ends, a tool: you know it when
you feel the subtle central turn or curve
that shapes it to the hand, was shaped by hands,
year after year after year, by women's hands
that held it here, just where it must be held
to fall of its own weight into the shallow bowl
and crush the seeds and rise and fall again
setting the rhythm of the soft, dull song
that worked itself at length into the stone,
so when I picked it up it told me how
to hold and heft it, put my fingers where
those fingers were that softly wore it down
to this fine shape that fits and fills my hand,
this weight that wants to fall and, falling, sing.

to the use of the word "technology" these days, is that people think "technology" means "high technology," resource-draining technology such as we delight in. And of course, a mortar and pestle is a very refined technology and a very useful one. All of our tools, the simplest tools, are technology, and a lot of them have been perfected—you can't improve upon them for what they do. A kitchen knife. It does what a kitchen knife does in human hands and you can't beat it. You can get an elaborate machine that slices meat for you and so on, but there you go. You're beginning to seek the save-time or don't-touch-it-yourself thing that high tech leads us toward. I just keep finding this, people saying, "You're antitechnology." Well, come off it. [Both laugh.] I write with a pen or pencil or on a computer. That's my job. I use technology all the time, but if I didn't have the computer or the pen or the pencil, I would end up scratching it on wood or stone or something.

DN: And it feels like the quote you have from Mary Jacobus, where she says that "the regulated speech of poetry may be as close as we can get to such things—to the stilled voice of the inanimate object or the insentient standing of trees," that perhaps this regulated speech is a form of technology also, to aid us in moving toward fellowship or contemplation.

UKL: I don't know if you can call language "technology." Technology is really involved with tools. Language is something we emit and we have to learn it at a certain period or we can't. Language is *strange*.

DN: In that same speech you talk about your mutual love of science and poetry, how science explicates and poetry implicates. Can you talk more about this, and about your desire to subjectify the universe? I know normally, when people think of subjectification, they think of something interior, maybe even self-referential, but here you're seeing it as a path toward reaching out.

UKL: There was an article by Frans de Waal in the *New York Times* about tickling bonobo apes and

. . .

Poetry is the human language that can try to say what a tree or a river *is,* that is, to speak humanly *for it,* in both senses of the word "for." A poem can do so by relating the quality of an individual human relationship to a thing, a rock or river or tree, or simply by describing the thing as truthfully as possible.

Science describes accurately from outside, poetry describes accurately from inside. Science explicates, poetry implicates. Both celebrate what they describe. We need the languages of both science and poetry to save us from merely stockpiling endless "information" that fails to inform our ignorance or our irresponsibility.

getting the complete, as it were, human response, of giggling, of drawing away but wanting more, and so on. A marvelous, subtle article. Many scientists want to objectify our relationship with animals and so we cannot say that the little ape is acting just the way a little human would. No, it's responding only in ape fashion. We mustn't use human words, we mustn't anthropomorphize. And as de Waal points out, there's this kind of terror of fellowship. We can't, we're not to, have fellow feeling with an ape or a mouse. But where's poetry without fellow feeling?

DN: You have a poem, "Contemplation at McCoy Creek," that deals with this issue of subjectifying the universe, of reaching outward, really well.

UKL: It's a kind of philosophical poem, and I will say a word about it. I was out in Harney County without a library, wondering what the word *contemplation* means. It seems to have the word *temple* in it, and the prefix *con* means "together," you know. So that is where I started, and then—this will explain the middle of the poem—there was a book in the ranch house, a kind of encyclopedia-dictionary, and it had a very good essay on the word *contemplation*. So it was sort of a learning experience, this poem.

DN: There is a line at the beginning of that poem— "seeking the sense within the word"—that reminded me of something you said in an interview with *Poetry Society of America*. They had a column called "First Loves," where they asked poets to talk about their first exposure to poetry. You talked about a collection of narrative poems, *Lays of Ancient Rome* by Thomas Babington Macaulay, and also about the poems of Swinburne, how you learned through those poems that you could tell stories through poems, but also that the stories are often beyond the meaning of the words themselves, that there is a deeper meaning of story that comes from the beat and the music of the words, not from the meaning of the individual words. Can you talk about that a little bit?

. . .

Contemplation at McCoy Creek

Seeking the sense within the word, I guessed:
        To be there in the sacred place,
the temple. To witness fully, and be thus
        the altar of the thing witnessed.

In shade beside the creek I contemplate
how the great waters coming from the heights
early this summer changed the watercourse.
The four big midstream boulders stayed in place.
The willows are some thriving and some dead,
rooted in, uprooted by the flood.
        Over the valley in the radiant light
a raven takes its way from east to west;
shadow wings across the rimrock pass
as silent as the raven. Contemplation
shows me nothing discontinuous.

When I looked in the book I found:
Time is the temple—Time itself and Space—
observed, marked out, to make the sacred place
on the four-quartered sky, the inwalled ground.

To join in continuity, the mind
        follows the water, shadows the birds,
observes the unmoved rock, the subtle flight.
        Slowly, in silence, without words,
the altar of the place and hour is raised.
Self is lost, a sacrifice to praise,
and praise itself sinks into quietness.

UKL: That deeper meaning is where poetry approaches music, because you cannot put that meaning in words in an intellectually comprehensible way. It's just there and you know it's there, and it is the rhythm and the beat, the music of the sound that carries it. This is extremely mysterious and rightly so.

DN: Robert Frost talks about it, or compares it to hearing somebody having a conversation on the other side of the wall. You're able to tell what they're saying through their intonation and their rhythm, but you don't actually hear any of the individual words.

UKL: You can tell what they're feeling, but you may not know really what they're talking about. You know how they feel about it by the sound—yeah, that's neat.

DN: When we last spoke, you also mentioned this with regard to Virginia Woolf, who I know didn't write much poetry. Is that a similar phenomenon, do you think, what you learned when you were young with poetry, around the meaning of the sound, and what you've described of the meaningfulness of Woolf's relation to sound when you write prose?

UKL: When you're talking about the sound in the rhythm of prose, it is so different from poetry, because it's in a way much coarser. It's a very *long* beat, the rhythms of a prose work. Of course, the sentence has its rhythms too. Woolf was intensely aware of that. She has a paragraph about how rhythm is what gives her the book, but, boy, it's hard to talk about. It's one of these experiential things that we don't really have a vocabulary for. I wonder if there is a vocabulary for it. It's like talking, again, about music. You can only say so much about music and then you simply have to play it. Some person can hear it and get it or not get it.

DN: Who are some of the poets that you love as an adult? Your cherished poets?

UKL: I have to put Rilke very high. I had MacIntyre's translation of *The Duino Elegies* one summer when I needed help. I was in a bad time, and I kind of feel like some of the elegies got me out of it. They carried me through it, anyway. I don't know German. So, Rilke and Goethe I have to get with facing translations and then just work my way back and forth and back and forth. Usually I end up trying to make my own crummy translation, so I can work my way into the German words with a dictionary. That is a very laborious way of reading poetry, but boy if you do it word by word, if you don't know the German nouns and have to look up every single one, and the verbs are mysterious and not in the right place [laughs], by the time you've done that, you know the poem. You've kind of made your own version of it in English, and that's why I love translating from languages I do know and even from languages I don't, like with Lao Tzu.

DN: You also wrote the preface to Rilke's *Poems from the Book of Hours* when New Directions rereleased it.

UKL: Actually *The Book of Hours* is not one of my favorites. I like later Rilke. He's a very strange poet and a lot of what he says doesn't mean much to me. But when he says things and it's the music, even I know. My father was a German speaker, and I heard him speak German, so I know what it sounds like even if I don't know the language. It's the music that carries it in reality. A strange rhythm he has.

DN: Can you talk about your attraction to translating Gabriela Mistral? You dedicate one of the poems in *Late in the Day* to her. What was it that you fell in love with?

UKL: It was not exactly love at first sight. I didn't know very much Spanish when I started reading her. My friend Diana Bellessi in Argentina sent me some selected Mistral and said, "You have to read this," and so I labored into it with my Spanish dictionary and I just fell in love. I never read anything like Mistral. There isn't anybody like Mistral, she's very

. . .

Muro

Muro fácil y extraordinario,
muro sin peso y sin color:
un poco de aire en el aire.

Pasan los pájaros de un sesgo,
pasa el columpio de la luz,
pasa el filo de los inviernos
como el resuello del verano;
pasan las hojas en las ráfagas
y las sombras incorporadas.

¡Pero no pasan los alientos,
pero el brazo no va a los brazos
y el pecho al pecho nunca alcanza!

Wall

Easy, extraordinary wall,
weightless wall, colorless,
a little air in the air.

Birds pass through it slantwise;
the swaying of the light,
the knife-edge of winter,
the sighs of summer pass across.
Storm-blown leaves can cross it
and embodied shadows.

But breath cannot get through,
arm cannot reach to reaching arms,
breast and breast can never meet.

individual, and it's an awful shame that Neruda—the other Chilean who got the Nobel—gets all the attention. But you know men tend to get the attention and you sort of struggle to keep the women in the eye of the men. Neruda is a very good poet, but Mistral just has a lot more to say to me than he does.

DN: And what about the endeavor of translating when you come back to your own writing? Do you feel like you can trace influences from the efforts of translation?

UKL: Oh, yeah. I can trace influences from individual poets and think, "Oh, I'm trying to do Rilke here, don't try that!" [Both laugh.]

DN: I really loved the afterword to *Late in the Day* entitled "Form, Free Verse, Free Form: Some Thoughts," where you talk about your long-standing poetry group, and also about the realization you had, from doing the poetry group assignments, that form can give you a poem. By that you don't mean to say that just by following the rules you're going to get a poem. You mean something else.

UKL: This is touching back on that same mystery of form, rhythm, and so on. This is something that I think is clear to many poets, but I was very slow to realize it. By committing yourself to a certain form— let's say a really complicated one, like a villanelle, which seems very artificial, and unbelievably difficult when you first approach it—certain lines are going to have to repeat themselves at certain intervals and you don't fiddle with that. If you write a villanelle, by golly, you write a villanelle. You don't write something like it and call it a villanelle. Take the rules seriously and somehow or other, as you follow them, you find that the necessity of having to do something gives you something to do. I don't know how that works, and it doesn't always work. The sonnet is probably the form most people think of when you talk about poetic form, and I find them terribly difficult. I write very, very few anymore. Maybe because there are so many very very good sonnets. I don't know, that doesn't usually worry me. It's just not a form that I work with very well. The quatrain, on the other hand, is a straight form in a way—just four lines, that's it. There's no other definition, but you can make it just as strict as you please with rhythm and rhyme and so on. I think any artist in any medium will tell you the same thing, that if you're working toward a certain form, whether you originated it or it's something you inherited from other artists, you have complete freedom there. In a way, I find metric rhyming verse gives me more freedom than free verse. It's a different kind of freedom.

DN: It reminds me of the fellowship with the pestle again, in a way. If you submit to a form, you're also entering a conversation with a history around the form as well.

UKL: There is that, yes, and that's exciting, although you *can't* think of it while you're writing, because that would be scary.

DN: You said in your *Paris Review* interview that, in fiction writing, you could also look at genre as a form, that sometimes by choosing to adopt a form in fiction, you will also discover things that you wouldn't have otherwise.

UKL: Absolutely. I think anybody who tries to write in genre seriously, who isn't just using it because it's chic at the moment or they think they could do better than hack writers, they find that "Oh, I have to do it this way, so how do I do that?" There's a sort of commitment there that makes you take it seriously. It opens up evidence to you that you would not have thought of by yourself, that the form hands over to you. But again, it's hard to describe.

DN: I'm curious about the absence or the relative absence of science fiction and fantasy in your poetry . . .

UKL: I can't put them together. There is a Science Fiction Poetry Association, and some poets that I grew up with, like Tennyson, were very good at doing a kind of science fictional poetry or putting science into their poetry. My mind apparently won't come together there. They're different businesses to me.

DN: In the afterword to *Late in the Day*, you talk about free form and free verse and how you do both. Can you talk more about free form? You mention Gerard Manley Hopkins as an example of someone taking a given form but altering it.

UKL: If you are a great enough poet you can make a curtal sonnet out of the sonnet. Sometimes I wonder about Gerard Manley Hopkins. I've never understood his sprung rhythm. I've tried and tried and tried. It doesn't make sense to me and I'm not quite sure that a curtal sonnet is a sonnet, but it's a lovely form. That was one of our assignments in my poetry group. I had to write one. I was terrified. [Both laugh.]

DN: I looked up the definition of a curtal sonnet and was quickly lost in the terminology of it. It is an eleven-line poem, but it consists precisely of three-fourths of the structure of a Petrarchan sonnet shrunk proportionally.

UKL: Yes. [Both laugh.] That's kind of a complex way of doing it, but yeah, and it has this very strange short last line. The rhyming is fairly complex, and that description didn't say that it's also broken into six lines and then five lines. There is a break, and that is similar to the classic sonnet, which has that turning in the middle.

DN: When you received the National Book Foundation Medal for Distinguished Contribution to American Letters in 2014, you gave both a beautiful and blistering speech about the commodification of art versus the practice of art. A speech that became an immediate viral sensation.

UKL: That was my fifteen minutes, my whole fifteen minutes. That was so amazing, when I woke up the next morning.

DN: You end *Late in the Day* with a transcript of this speech. In it you say that resistance and change often begin in art, and that most often it is in the art of words that you see the beginnings of resistance and change.

UKL: After all, dictators are always afraid of poets. This seems kind of weird to a lot of Americans to whom poets are not political beings, but it doesn't seem a bit weird in South America or in any dictatorship, really.

ON NONFICTION

Over the past decade, it is in-the-world Ursula, as public figure and public thinker that has risen to prominence. During that time, she publicly resigned from the Authors Guild to protest the settlement with Google that allowed them to digitize books in disregard of copyright. She also gave what is widely regarded as the most ferocious speech in National Book Foundation history, using her acceptance of the Medal of Distinguished Contribution to American Letters to lambast the deepening corporatization and commodification of books and their authors by the likes of Amazon. She has become an important part of the national conversation on many issues of the day, from the meaning of facts in the so-called postfactual era, to the meaning of "public lands" at a time when a wildlife refuge in southeastern Oregon was occupied by a militia in order to "liberate" such lands from the government. It is also during this time that Ursula has opened up about her early struggles as a writer, offered advice on writing in a website forum, and given us a different look into her life with the serial publication of her cat Pard's "memoirs" on her blog.

It seemed fitting, then, for our third conversation, one about writing nonfiction, that we met not at the radio station, but at her home. Erin, the PM news coordinator at KBOO, someone who coincidentally was helping with a documentary being filmed on Ursula's life and career, volunteered to serve as sound engineer for our conversation. I traveled there with Erin, and we set up in a cozy book-filled space on the upper floor of the house where the sound quality would be at its best for a field recording. Nevertheless, the outside world still intervened. We paused as a truck rumbled by on a nearby street, or to greet Pard, who wanted to check out what all the fuss was about before returning to his favored spot on the bed in a nearby bedroom.

You'll discover, as I did, that Ursula feels most at home in fiction and poetry, more uneasy in the world of declaration and assertion. In her novel *The Left Hand of Darkness*, she writes, "To learn which questions are unanswerable, and *not to answer them*: this skill is most needful in times of stress and darkness." And yet, in her essay collections, her literary criticism, her speeches—this arena where she delivers her views on things—whether about science and the environment, Google and Amazon, or feminism and the canon, she seems to do so in defense of the voiceless and in the spirit of the unanswerable inside every artist, every person.

At the end of this nonfiction conversation, I mentioned how rare it is to be able to talk with someone with such a deep history in all three genres—fiction, poetry, nonfiction. How unique this journey had been. In fact, I couldn't imagine who else I could've done this with. "Maybe we should make this into a book!" Ursula answered. And here we are, her musing has become our reality, an object out in the world, held open in our hands.

—David Naimon

• • •

DAVID NAIMON: This is our third conversation about your writing, the first two times at the radio station and this time here at your house. Given that we've talked about both fiction and poetry, when Small Beer Press announced its release of your collection of nonfiction, it seemed only natural to complete the circle, the circle of genres, to meet again, to talk about the art of the essay, and the art of literary criticism. It's interesting, however, that when a reader opens *Words Are My Matter* for the first time, the first thing they will encounter is a poem followed by the first sentence of the foreword, where you say: "I seldom have as much pleasure in reading nonfiction as I do a poem or a story." Can you elaborate on why that is? And why you open the book with an interrogation of your interest, or lack of interest, in nonfiction?

URSULA K. LE GUIN: I don't know that I can explain it. This is my fourth or fifth book of nonfiction but, in fact, I don't think of myself as a nonfiction writer. So I suppose it was a backhanded apology in a way. Here I am doing this again, even though I'm saying, "It's not my thing, it's not really my shtick." But here I am, waving it around.

DN: So, as a reader, what is the nonfiction that you gravitate toward? What in your mind elevates a work of nonfiction to a type of art that is compelling to you?

UKL: It's what I find I *can* read. It partly has to do, I think, with old age. I need a narrative, but I've always really needed a narrative. I'm just no good at abstract thinking. That means I tend to read biography and autobiography, and sciences such as geology, which tell a story through history, and history itself. And not very much that is abstract or theoretical. I have real trouble with philosophy. I took it as a freshman in college. We all had to. And I liked it but it never would stick. I can't keep it in my head. It has to be a story. If it is a parable then I remember it.

DN: You said in the foreword to *Words Are My Matter* something that you alluded to here as well. You said that writing fiction and poetry is natural for you, you desire to do it and are fulfilled by doing it and feel like you can judge its honesty and its quality in a way that you can't with your nonfiction. That writing nonfiction feels like work, and that, unlike your stories, it will be judged by people who know a lot more than you do about whatever the topic is at hand. Given that unnerving uncertainty how do you ultimately find solid ground and know an essay is finished and stands on sturdy legs?

UKL: Getting started is hard. I throw away endless first pages grinding the gears until I can get the machinery going. As for knowing when it's done, that's a real poser sometimes. I wrote a piece for a talk years ago, "The Fisherwoman's Daughter," and every time I gave it as a talk the audience would give me so much feedback that I'd have to rewrite the article. Finally I just said, "Enough! I have to stop rewriting it!" and published it as it was. But doing that means you didn't finish something per se, you just had to stop. And I feel that, for any piece that is a matter of opinion, you really have to try to leave the door open at the end of the piece.

DN: You name one particular essay in the book, entitled "Living in a Work of Art," as perhaps your favorite piece in the collection. And it is one of the rare pieces that wasn't commissioned. It was something you wanted to write, on the pure principle of it. You say something very interesting about the process of writing this piece: "When I can use prose as I do in writing stories as a direct means or form of thinking, not as a way of saying something I know or believe, not as a vehicle for a message, but as an exploration, a voyage of discovery resulting in something I didn't know before I wrote it, then I feel that I am using it properly." I would love it if you could tell us a little about the process of exploration in putting together "Living in a Work of Art," because I know, as a reader of it, one of the pleasures was the sense of exploring with you, of discovering things as you were discovering them.

UKL: Probably that piece is as near to autobiography as I'm going to come. It goes back to my childhood, to a house that I left when I was seventeen, though I stayed there as a visitor for many years. So I was thinking back a long way—part of what is going on is an old woman exploring her childhood. What about this place where I lived, which simply was home, the universe for me when I was little? I was trying to explore what it was like, the ramifications and meanings of that, how that house shaped me. And I know it did. And then there was the simple pleasure of writing about this house that I loved so dearly. Being there and thinking about it.

. . .

I don't know what novel our Maybeck house could be compared to, but it would contain darkness and radiant light; its beauty would arise from honest, bold, inventive construction, from geniality and generosity of spirit and mind, and would also have elements of fantasy and strangeness.

Writing this, I wonder if much of my understanding of what a novel ought to be was taught to me, ultimately, by living in that house. If so, perhaps all my life I have been trying to rebuild it around me out of words.

DN: You grew up in a house built by a remarkable architect, Bernard Maybeck. One of the things that struck me in reading this essay about it was how you talked about the house being built in anticipation of its future inhabitants, as if the imagination of the architect is creating a space for people he hasn't yet met.

UKL: When Maybeck planned a house he was imagining the family that might live in it. He was not designing a "machine for living," or expressing his ego, as so many architects do and are praised for doing. He was doing anything but, and yet "Maybecks" are instantly recognizable. One thing I didn't know when I started writing the essay was that Maybeck had expressed himself so clearly about what he saw as his goals as an architect. It was very useful to me, very interesting, and I hadn't known it. He was a quiet person. The ego was not huge and formidable the way it is with the "star-chitects," as they call them.

DN: We've talked before, when we were talking about fiction and poetry, about the role of the ego, the role of the intellect being secondary, in service of something more mysterious. We talked about the deeper meaning of the words, beyond their definitions, the meaning that comes from the syntax, the music of their arrangement, the "wave in the mind," as you called it, citing Virginia Woolf. And also the way Taoism and Buddhism, the way *wu wei*, or not-doing, has informed some of your poetry. Hearing you talk about this architect, and his approach to building your house that is not ego-directed, that perhaps was built with a similar ethos to how your own writing is constructed, I wonder if this is where the split comes for you around nonfiction, that so much of nonfiction is ego-driven, so much of it is about saying what you believe or think.

UKL: Yes, saying what you think *explicitly*. Not being able to sneak around it and imply it. This tends to lead me toward . . . sometimes ranting. Being overexplicit and defensive.

DN: Perhaps the most polar opposite essay in the collection from "Living in a Work of Art" is your speech you gave when you received the National Book Foundation medal in 2014. It's the most polar opposite in the sense that you were asked to deliver a message.

UKL: I think they just asked me to say thank you. [Laughs.] But if you have a message it is a chance. You've got six minutes. They can't stop you!

DN: I read that you spent six months reworking this six-minute speech, and hadn't felt that nervous delivering a speech since you were in junior high. Tell us a little more about this anxiety and uncertainty that motivated the reworking of this speech prior to delivering it.

UKL: I figure, "Okay, I've got six minutes." And I am talking to some of the powers that be in American literature in that room in New York. All my publishers were there. And there was an Amazon table, and all the rest of them. So I felt an onus upon me to say something meaningful. But how to say it in a very brief time without it being just a rant? Because I have strong feelings about what has been happening in literature, particularly in certain aspects of publishing, how certain things were going in the absolutely wrong direction. I wanted to talk about this. And then there is the sense that we all have, and of course we have it more intensely since the election, that the times are changing very fast. And they are very unpredictable and pretty scary. Whatever may happen to the arts in bad times, the verbal arts, at least, tend to become very important. It's really important what you say in the bad times. I think about a book that has been so important to me, Lao Tzu's *Tao Te Ching*. That book is the product of a very bad time in China. It was called the Warring States Period. A time of civil war and invasion. And he was, in fact, going into exile. In the mythology about him, that was why he wrote the book. Staying at an inn on the border, before he crossed over into "the outer world," he took a night or two to write this book. So, I thought, okay, you do your testimony when things are getting bad. And I wanted to do that. I needed to figure out what I really, really wanted to say.

DN: And for people who might not be aware, your speech became a viral phenomenon and giant news story around the globe.

UKL: Yeah, it was my fifteen minutes of fame. I was completely taken aback. I really thought nobody would be listening except for the people in that room. But I forgot that a lot of the people in that room were journalists and knew a story when they heard one.

DN: After this discussion of your views on the positioning of the mind and the ego in relationship to art, I returned to the poem at the beginning of *Words Are My Matter*, entitled "The Mind Is Still." It begins: "The mind is still. The gallant books of lies / are never quite enough. / Ideas are a whirl of mazy flies / over the pigs' trough." It seems particularly fitting now looking at it through this lens.

UKL: I hope so. The title for the book comes from that poem. It was written quite a long time ago, so I hoped it would make sense in context.

DN: If we are looking at the different ways your work is received in relationship to ideas and the mind, you have this really interesting essay about your book *The Dispossessed*, one of your more well-known novels. You talk about some of the scholarly work around this novel and say that you resist the idea that novels spring from an originating idea, also the idea that science fiction is the literature of ideas, and that you'd rather be prasied for your efforts to resist the didactic than for your failures to do so. Did this arise from a dissatisfaction with how *The Dispossesed* was being received, or how it was being discussed in scholarly works?

UKL: No, not really. Actually, that essay was written as an introduction for a book, a collection of essays, about the novel *The Disposssessed*. I was kind of amazed to discover most of those discussions were not only highly intelligent and professional but also simpatico, using feeling as well as idea. I have nothing against ideas per se—I am an intellectual, after all—but when they become didactic, self-righteous, or just opinion then they get tiresome. What I was struggling against was not the reception of *The Dispossessed* in particular, though it is often treated as if there is nothing in it but ideas, but the tendency to intellectualize not only science fiction but all literature. It is often taught with questions like "What is the author saying?" and "What is his message?" [Sighs with exasperation.] Any work of art consists of more than verbal thoughts that can be paraphrased verbally. There is something more going on that has got to be included in the criticism. You can't reduce any novel or poem to an intelligible single meaning.

DN: In "The Operating Instructions," which comes from a 2002 talk at a meeting of Oregon Literary Arts, you write really wonderfully about an American-specific fear of imagination. In one of our past talks I mistakenly confused this with our resistance to considering genre fiction as literature. I wondered then if, now that genre fiction was finally breaking those walls down, that meant America was coming to terms with imagination in a healthier way. You pushed back and said that the question of America and imagination is a bigger and broader one than the question of genre fiction and literature but we never went further at the time. What is it about the American spirit that makes us fearful of the imaginative spirit?

UKL: That old essay is called "Why Are Americans Afraid of Dragons?" and it was written specifically about the American tendency to dismiss all fantasy, all highly imaginative fiction, as for kids, or as unimportant because it isn't about what the stock market is doing today. The immediate profit attitude toward

"The Operating Instructions"

· · ·

A poet has been appointed ambassador. A playwright is elected president. Construction workers stand in line with office managers to buy a new novel. Adults seek moral guidance and intellectual challenge in stories about warrior monkeys, one-eyed giants, and crazy knights who fight windmills. Literacy is considered a beginning, not an end

. . . Well, maybe in some other country, but not this one. In America the imagination is generally looked on as something that might be useful when the TV is out of order. Poetry and plays have no relation to practical politics. Novels are for students, housewives, and other people who don't work. Fantasy is for children and primitive peoples. Literacy is so you can read the operating instructions. I think the imagination is the single most useful tool mankind possesses. It beats the opposable thumb. I can imagine living without my thumbs, but not without my imagination.

life. Dickens talks about it in his novel *Hard Times*, making fun of the completely "realistic" businessman who can't think of anything but immediate use and profit and therefore loses any sense of there really being any future. This mind-set, as it comes through in education (Dickens was very clear about that too), is crippling to a child's whole development. Because the imagination is simply a very large part of the way our minds function. To stint or stunt or be contemptuous of the imagination is a terrible thing to do, particularly to a young developing mind that needs to be able to think about anything—to imagine things, and be clear about the difference between what is imagined and what is real. I think children are much better at that than most adults give them credit for. They know when it is a fairy tale. And they often know when it is a lie. But still, both reason and imagination need training. They need exercise just like the body does. We train some of the rational faculties, but less and less is the imaginative given any place in American education. I think that is very scary.

DN: You say something in your talk "The Operating Instructions" that fascinates me. That "home" isn't your family, nor is the house where you live. Home is instead imaginary. And by imaginary you don't mean illusory, but in some respects more real than any other place. You write, "Home, imagined, comes to be. It is real, realer than any other place, but you can't get to it unless your people show you how to imagine it—whoever your people are." Can you unpack that a little for us, the ways humans imagine "home," create groups, invent ways to live, and imagine as a means of thriving?

UKL: A function of myth in what we used to call "primitive" societies, real myth as told seriously by serious grown-ups to others, perhaps one of its main functions, is telling us who we are. For instance, "We are the Diné," or "We are the Apache." And a very large part of knowing who we are is knowing where we came from, where we live now, and if there is a further home to go to, what might it be? Placing yourself among your people within a certain context on the Earth. And it seems to take a lively effort of the imagination to accomplish this, so all myths in a sense are "unrealistic." And yet they are trying to get to the heart of one's reality as a human being who is a member of a community. Which is kind of an important job.

DN: Right after this investigation of the imagination in the book we come across a talk you gave at the Conference on Literature and Ecology in 2005 called "The Beast in the Book," where you talk about imagination in relationship to nature and the non-human other. You talk about the coexistence of animal and human in story, in folktales, fairy tales, and fables, about how only in the postindustrial age are animal tales considered only for children. It makes me think about one of the taboos in literary fiction, one that you see explicitly prohibited in the guidelines of many literary magazines, that of stories that have talking animals, or that are told from the imagined perspective of an animal. Do you think this limiting of the animal to children is a postindustrial phenomenon or an American postindustrial phenomenon?

UKL: It's not just American. It includes European literature too. The thing is we don't live with animals as we did. The relationship has changed immensely in the last two hundred years. You didn't used to be able to get away from the animals. They were part of your life, absolutely essential to your well-being as fellow workers in the field, as your food supply, your wool supply, and so on. Now we get all that at an enormous distance. Now there are people who can't be in a room with an animal. What would they have done a hundred years ago? I really don't know. They would have to like it or lump it, I guess. Children grow up never touching any living being except another human being. No wonder we are alienated. We can live in the cities as if there were no other living beings on Earth. No wonder people get indifferent and think it doesn't matter if you extinguish a species. You have to be in

111

"The Beast in the Book"

. . .

Why do most children and many adults respond both to real animals and to stories about them, fascinated by and identifying with creatures which our dominant religions and ethics consider more objects for human use: no longer working with us, in industrial societies, but mere raw material for our food, subjects of scientific experiments to benefit us, entertaining curiosities of the zoo and the TV nature program, pets kept to improve our psychological health?

Perhaps we give animal stories to children and encourage their interest in animals because we see children as inferior, mentally "primitive," not yet fully human: so we see pets and zoos and animal stories as "natural" steps on the child's way up to adult, exclusive humanity—rungs on the ladder from mindless, helpless babyhood to the full glory of intellectual maturity and mastery. Ontogeny recapitulating phylogeny in terms of the Great Chain of Being.

But what is it the kid is after—the baby wild with excitement at the sight of a kitten, the six-year-old spelling out *Peter Rabbit*, the twelve-year-old weeping as she reads *Black Beauty*? What is it the child perceives that her whole culture denies?

touch and we are not. I think that kids' stories and animal stories are an imaginative way at least of being in touch. Therefore they are very important. But my opinion is not shared by a lot of literary people. Literary people tend to assume if it is about animals, it is probably sentimental. And sentimentality is the worst possible sin.

DN: Well, here at your house, during this conversation, another author has been coming in and out of the room. Your cat Pard has a new book out himself. Tell us a little bit about Pard's nonfiction.

UKL: [Laughs.] I shamelessly—and really there's a shamelessness to it—pretended I was Pard and wrote his autobiography. I say shameless because what I think and feel is *immensely* different than what Pard thinks and feels. I humanized him completely. But I hope it's not what is called colonialism. I hope I am not just co-opting Pard. I have a great deal of respect for him. I attempted to share with others what I do understand, or can guess, about his feelings. And no more than that. This whole thing about writing about the other—animals are just the tip of the iceberg.

DN: Speaking of that, you bring up a book, T. H. White's *The Sword in the Stone*, as an important book, and it was one that was hugely important to me growing up. Mainly because of the different animals Merlin turns the future King Arthur into as part of his education.

UKL: Arthur gets to be all kinds of creatures—a hawk, a hedgehog—even a rock. It is absolutely wonderful. It had a deep, permanent effect on me, too. Unfortunately, when White incorporated *The Sword in the Stone* into *The Once and Future King*, he left out some of the very best of it—cut marvelous, mystical things, added political rants. Most people who know both think it was a mistake, and you should get the old book if you can find it.

DN: Later you say, "We human beings have made a world reduced to ourselves and our artifacts but we aren't made for it." This feels kind of like a tragic horror story of sorts, that we've created a world and then a literature about that world that we are ill-suited to, one that references only ourselves.

UKL: We are suited to live in it, but it is such a small part of the world we could be living in. Let's put it that way. It makes it less of a horror story and more of an existential mistake.

DN: Taking that a step further, I wonder if the resistance to considering fantasy or science fiction as literature is partly because of the elevation of the non-human in it, of the decentralization of humanity with regard to intelligence or otherwise.

UKL: You are right on it there. There is real resistance to this. And this is behind a lot of the resistance to science. Because science—not just Copernicus, most science—moves us away from the center of things. Because we aren't. You find out how unimaginably old the Earth is and you feel sort of dethroned. Many people can't bear it. They hate it. It makes them feel alienated. That's the pity of it. If they could get into it, science could give them a much deeper sense of identification with all these marvelous processes that are going on all around us all the time, that we are part of. All of us.

DN: You write a lot about gender, sexism, feminism, and gendered literature in this collection and there is a talk you gave at the Winter Fishtrap, the gathering in Joseph, Oregon, called: "What Women Know," where you resist making a cult of women's knowledge, of associating women with the instinctual, with nature, with the dark, because it reinforces the masculinist idea of women as more primitive. Reading this I felt a subtextual conversation going on between "What Women Know" and "The Beast in the Book." Together they seem like a call both to bring the nonhuman other, to bring nature and animals back into literature but also to decouple the idea that the realm of nature is the realm of women. Instead you imagine a world where men spend some time in the darkness that they avoid and women up in the light, that women claim their rightful place in the world of reason and ideas and action too. I'd love for you to unpack this a little more for us, your interrogation of the gendered nature of nature.

UKL: I suppose it comes down in some ways to the brute and simple fact that a woman conceives, carries a child, and bears it. Women can perform this enormous natural act that men can't. So how much of this is male compensation? How much of a lot of human behavior is male compensation, claiming generative power as the only power, and calling any other power or ability inferior? That is a theme that goes through a lot of my writing, because it goes through a lot of our lives.

DN: In a previous conversation we talked about the erasure of women writers from the canon, or women not being considered for the canon in the first place. We talked about Grace Paley as one example since she passed away, and also about C. J. Cherryh in relation to William Gibson, how they were both winning awards at the same time, both seeming to shape the conversation of the moment, but flash forward a couple of decades and everyone knows who William Gibson is and far fewer people have even heard of Cherryh. So I was happy to see your essay in *Words Are My Matter* called "Disappearing Grandmothers," where you enumerate four ways women are erased from the canon, or diminished in the conversation of literature: denigration, omission, exception, and disappearance.

You took the title "Disappearing Grandmothers" from a letter of Wallace Stegner's. The story you relate about Wallace Stegner, and what he did to the writer Mary Foote, was quite a shocking tale, and an egregious example of the disappearance of a woman writer.

. . .

Exception

A novel by a man is very seldom discussed with any reference to the author's gender. A novel by a woman is very frequently discussed with reference to her gender. The norm is male. The woman is an exception to the norm, from which she is excluded.

Exception and exclusion are practiced both in criticism and in reviewing. A critic forced to admit that, say, Virginia Woolf is a great English novelist may take pains to show her as an exception—a wonderful fluke. Techniques of exception and exclusion are manifold. The woman writer is found not to be in the "mainstream" of English novels; her writing is "unique" but has no influence on later writers; she is the object of a "cult"; she is a (charming, elegant, poignant, sensitive, fragile) hothouse flower that should not be seen as competing with the (rugged, powerful, masterful) vigor of the male novelist.

Joyce was almost instantly canonized; Woolf was either excluded from the canon or admitted grudgingly and with reservations for decades. It is quite arguable that *To the Lighthouse*, with its subtle and effective narrative techniques and devices, has been far more influential on later novel-writing than *Ulysses*, which is a monumental dead end. Joyce, choosing "silence, exile, cunning," led a sheltered life, taking responsibility for nothing but his own writing and career. Woolf led a fully engaged life in her own country in an extraordinary circle of intellectually, sexually, and politically active people; and she knew, read, reviewed, and published other authors all her grown life. Joyce is the fragile person, Woolf the tough one; Joyce is the cult object and the fluke, Woolf the continuously fertile influence, central to the twentieth-century novel.

But centrality is the last thing accorded a woman by the canoneers. Women must be left on the margins.

Even when a woman novelist is admitted to be a first-rate artist, the techniques of exclusion still operate. Jane Austen is vastly admired, yet she is less often considered as an exemplar than as unique, inimitable—a wonderful fluke. She cannot be dis-appeared; but she is not fully included.

Denigration, omission, and exception during a writer's lifetime are preparations for her disappear-ance after her death.

UKL: Mary Foote was a novelist and short story writer of no particular literary distinction but some popularity. She wrote some very good stories. Fairly well-known in her own lifetime, which was basically two generations before Wallace Stegner's. She wrote a very fine autobiography, which was not published during her lifetime. [Note: It was published in 1972 under the silly and misleading title *A Victorian Gentlewoman in the Far West*.] Stegner was given a copy of this book and some of Foote's letters by her grandchildren. He took it and built his novel *Angle of Repose* on it, on her book, her life story. I believe he took even his title from it. It's a geologist's term. It's the angle of a hill at which a rock can come to rest. Beautiful title. And the only credit he gave to Mary Hallock Foote was to thank her grandchildren for the "loan" of their grandmother. He didn't even name her. I hold this as unforgiveable. I cannot forgive Wallace Stegner, who was very well-known, very popular, very much adored by the intelligentsia, who easily could afford to give credit where credit was due. And he didn't. I do not forgive.

DN: Back when we were talking about imagining the inner life of your cat, you mentioned some of the possible pitfalls of writing across difference. You participated in a project with Pharos Editions where authors were asked to pick an out-of-print book that they felt particularly deserved to be back in print and you chose a book by Charles L. McNichols called *Crazy Weather*, a book you read as a teenager and then some seventy years later. It raises some interesting questions about writing across difference too, given that McNichols is white and writing about the Mojave people and their myths. Writing across difference has been a hot topic in the literary world the last couple of years, with Lionel Shriver's notorious speech asserting her right to do whatever she wants regardless of how it is received, a speech she gave while provocatively wearing a Mexican sombrero, as just the latest part of that ongoing conversation. What are your thoughts on writing across difference, writing as a different race, gender, or otherwise, the risks and potential rewards of it?

UKL: Oh, David, that's a real can of worms. People have been talking about this for decades now. How far can you speak for a person of a culture not your own? My father was an anthropologist and ran smack into this. When does an attempt to understand become co-optation? This was of course extremely, egregiously visible when white people wrote in the person of Indians, from Fenimore Cooper on. They were co-opting the voice of the Indians, who had no literary voice at that time, but certainly had their own oral literature, their own voice and their own opinions. Those went unheard. They had to be interpreted through the whites. This goes on. Men have been speaking for women for thousands of years, when women had no voice whatsoever, in literature or anywhere else. And that still goes on. But then, okay, if you politicize that to the extent that you say nobody can speak for anybody else, then you get into a mess. Because what we need to say is nobody can speak for anybody who doesn't have a voice. Of course this is where it gets sticky with animals. Of course, they don't have a voice. That is their being.

They don't use language as we do. So to what extent can we speak for them? To a very limited extent. On the other hand you don't have to be like the behavior scientists who say that because we don't understand their feelings they don't have any, because we don't understand how they think they don't think. Or even to say, as Wittgenstein does, that if a lion could talk we wouldn't understand him. That's not necessarily true. But all we can do is imagine our way into the other. And be very, very, very careful at every step, that we are not co-opting that other. Taking it over and putting our voice where we are trying to imagine what its voice is or would be. Eternal vigilance is required.

DN: And you put forth Charles L. McNichol's *Crazy Weather* as a relatively successful example of doing this well.

UKL: I did and I was taking a deliberate risk there. I know how the Indians feel about the whites speaking for them and they are absolutely justified in every respect. And yet I picked this book which is a white man writing in the voice of a person who is not an Indian, but a boy who was brought up by the Mojave. I have to assume that to some extent McNichol was. He couldn't have known it that well otherwise. He just couldn't have talked from inside that way. And since the book has an introduction by an Indian grandmother, totally approving, I felt like he did it right. He did it carefully, without co-opting. The sense that you are in touch with something really different—completely human and extremely understandable emotionally—but really different. That's one of the great things novels do.

DN: One of the sections of *Words Are My Matter* contains your introductions to a variety of different books and also notes on different writers. We learn some interesting facts about you as we read them, for instance, that you and Philip K. Dick went to the same high school at the same time but never knew each other and that you refused your Nebula Award in the 1970s as a protest against the Science Fiction Writers of America revoking Stanislaw Lem's honorary membership because of Cold War politics. And that the award was then given to Isaac Asimov, a cold warrior.

UKL: Served me right for being self-righteous, I guess.

DN: Among all the writers you engage with in this section, I was hoping we could talk about José Saramago and his importance to you in particular. In this book we get notes about him as a writer and also several book reviews and you say that he is the only novelist of your generation whom you still learn from. Tell us a little about what makes Saramago of such ongoing importance to you.

UKL: It all began with the poet Naomi Replansky, who is now ninety-nine and lives in New York, whom I got to know as a pen pal. Naomi was reading one of Saramago's novels, *Blindness*, and told me, "This is great, you've got to read this." So I got a copy, because I obey Naomi, and it scared me to death. I just couldn't read it. It was so

Conversations on Writing

frightening and it was extremely difficult to read because there is no paragraphing and very little punctuation. It is made almost as if to deliberately slow you down. I backed off but I could feel there was something here. So I went and got some more Saramago and put myself through a course on his work. This is all within the last ten or fifteen years, very late in my life. He is not very far ahead of me. He was maybe ten years older than me. He started writing novels very late in his life and he was still writing novels in his seventies and eighties. That's not only impressive but good news to me. You don't have to stop. So I invested a lot in Saramago and it paid off for me. He is not an easy writer, partly because of his idiosyncratic punctuation and paragraphing. You just have to allow him that. I still don't quite understand why he does it but I have to figure that any artist that good knows why he did it. He was very far left, a Marxist, not a devout Marxist, a socialist, always against the dictatorship in his home country, Portugal, and always against the heavy hand of the Catholic Church there. A man of extreme moral sensitivity, and terrific sympathy for

129

all kinds of underdogs, including women and dogs. He won my heart is what happened. Boy, the Nobel committee made a good choice that time—otherwise I never would have heard of him. Most of us wouldn't have. Being Portuguese is damnation as a writer. It takes a lot to get you out of writing in a "minor" language. Because he was always translated into Spanish, immediately, I think, he might slowly have come to notice. But I'm happy they Nobel-ed him.

DN: We've talked before about your book reviews. I think they are particularly interesting to read for writers and aspiring writers, as they become lessons in different areas of craft. I think your reviews of David Mitchell's *The Bone Clocks*, China Miéville's *Embassytown*, and Curtis Sittenfeld's *Eligible* are particularly memorable in this regard. You definitely don't pull your punches in your reviews but one thing I noticed that particularly gets your goat is when writers who are not from the world of science fiction and fantasy do a poor job with regard to acknowledging or understanding the tropes of the genre. I think of your review of Cormac McCarthy's *The Road* and Chang-Rae Lee's *On Such a Full Sea* as two recent examples that seemed to exasperate you.

UKL: I didn't actually review *The Road*. I just took a crack at it while reviewing the book by Chang Rae Lee.

DN: What are some of the common pitfalls or particular annoyances you have with writers who try their hand at sci-fi or fantasy from outside the field?

UKL: They haven't read any science fiction. They have no idea really what it can do or what it's about. What tends to happen is that they laboriously reinvent the wheel. They get an idea, which is a commonplace idea in science fiction, one that has been worked over a thousand times, worked over with all kinds of literary variations, but because science fiction was not taught as literature they don't know that. They take this old well-worn idea and bring it forth, declaring, "Look! Look at this wonderful idea I had!"

DN: You had a reverse scenario with reviewing Margaret Atwood's *The Year of the Flood*. Atwood is a writer you greatly admire, and she is considered one of the great living science fiction writers, but she herself insists she does not write science fiction. You felt like this insistence put some constraints on how you could approach your review of the book. Can you talk a little bit about this challenge for you, of assessing Atwood's work in this review?

UKL: She excepts her work from being science fiction because she defines science fiction very narrowly. Science fiction to her is really more fantasy. It is things that can't happen on Earth and things that are not happening on Earth. Sorry, Maggie, but that doesn't define science fiction. A lot of it is very much about what is happening on Earth right now. It often extrapolates a little from that and really that's what her science fiction does. She takes the way things are going, particularly politically, on Earth and extrapolates it into the future and goes, "Oh my god, it is going to be like this," which is pretty dire. But that's just an old science fiction technique. I don't know why she doesn't want her books to be called science fiction. But it's not too hard to imagine some of the reasons. One of them is that her publishers absolutely didn't want them to be called that, as that would make her a "genre writer." And she wouldn't sell as well. But Margaret Atwood is far too bright and complicated a person to be motivated by anything that crass. But it does make for a considerable discomfort sometimes in our ongoing conversation as writers who like each other. I just insist that when I write science fiction I know what it is and I know that I'm writing it. And I'm not going to have it called anything else. But that also is true when I'm not writing science fiction. I don't want it called science fiction just because I'm a "science fiction writer." These categories are very, very important to me personally. I'm always kind of on thin ice when trying to review Atwood. But it is always interesting.

DN: Maybe this is a good time to have you read "On Serious Literature."

UKL: [Flips through pages of the book.] Oh! [Laughs.] I couldn't think what it was! This piece is a response to a review by Ruth Franklin in *Slate* in May of 2007. She wrote of the book she was reviewing: "Michael Chabon has spent considerable energy trying to drag the decaying corpse of genre fiction out of the shallow grave where writers of serious literature abandoned it." And this is my response:

. . .

Something woke her in the night. Was it steps she heard, coming up the stairs—somebody in wet training shoes, climbing the stairs very slowly . . . but who? And why wet shoes? It hadn't rained. There, again, the heavy, soggy sound. But it hadn't rained for weeks, it was only sultry, the air close, with a cloying hint of mildew or rot, sweet rot, like very old finiocchiona, or perhaps liverwurst gone green. There, again—the slow, squelching, sucking steps, and the foul smell was stronger. Something was climbing her stairs, coming closer to her door. As she heard the click of heel bones that had broken through rotting flesh, she knew what it was. But it was dead, dead! God damn that Chabon, dragging it out of the grave where she and the other serious writers had buried it to save serious literature from its polluting touch, the horror of its blank, pustular face, the lifeless, meaningless glare of its decaying eyes! What did the fool think he was doing? Had he paid no attention at all to the endless rituals of the serious writers and their serious critics—the formal expulsion ceremonies, the repeated anathemata, the stakes driven over and over through the heart, the vitriolic sneers, the endless, solemn dances on the grave? Did he not want to preserve the virginity of Yaddo? Had he not even understood the importance of the distinction between sci fi and counterfactual fiction? Could he not see that Cormac McCarthy—although everything in his book (except the wonderfully blatant use of an egregiously obscure vocabulary) was remarkably similar to a great many earlier works of science fiction about men crossing the country after a holocaust—could never under any circumstances be said to be a sci fi writer, because Cormac McCarthy was a serious writer and so *by definition* incapable of lowering himself to commit genre? Could it be that that Chabon, just because some mad fools gave him a Pulitzer, had forgotten the sacred value of the word mainstream? No, she would not look at the thing that had squelched its way into her bedroom and stood over her, reeking of rocket fuel and kryptonite, creaking like an old mansion on the moors in a wuthering wind, its brain rotting like a pear from within, dripping little grey cells through its ears. But its call on her attention was, somehow, imperative, and as it stretched out its hand to her she saw on one of the half-putrefied fingers a fiery golden ring. She moaned. How could they have buried it in such a shallow grave and then just walked away, abandoning it? "Dig it deeper, dig it deeper!" she had screamed, but they hadn't listened to her, and now where were they, all the other serious writers and critics, when she needed them? Where was her copy of *Ulysses*? All she had on her bedside table was a Philip Roth novel she had been using to prop up the reading lamp. She pulled the slender volume free and raised it up between her and the ghastly golem—but it was not enough. Not even Roth could save her. The monster laid its squamous hand on her, and the ring branded her like a burning coal. Genre breathed its corpse-breath in her face, and she was lost. She was defiled. She might as well be dead. She would never, ever get invited to write for *Granta* now.

DN: I just adore that piece, Ursula.

UKL: It's pretty mean, isn't it?

DN: It must've been so fun to write.

UKL: It was. It was. Revenge is sweet!

URSULA K. LE GUIN published twenty-one novels, eleven volumes of short stories, four collections of essays, twelve books for children, six volumes of poetry and four of translation, and has received the Hugo, Nebula, Endeavor, Locus, Tiptree, Sturgeon, PEN/ Malamud, and National Book awards and the Pushcart and Janet Heidinger Kafka prizes, among others.

In recent years she has received lifetime achievement awards from the World Fantasy Awards, *Los Angeles Times*, Pacific Northwest Booksellers Association, and Willamette Writers, as well as the Science Fiction and Fantasy Writers of America Grand Master Award, the Library of Congress "Living Legend" award, and the National Book Foundation Medal for Distinguished Contribution to American Letters. Le Guin was the recipient of the Association for Library Service to Children's May Hill Arbuthnot Honor Lecture Award and the Margaret Edwards Award. She lived in Portland, Oregon, and her website is www.ursulakleguin.com.

DAVID NAIMON is a writer and the host of the radio show and podcast *Between the Covers* in Portland, Oregon. His work has appeared in *Tin House, AGNI, Fourth Genre, Boulevard, ZYZZYVA*, and elsewhere. His writing has been reprinted in *The Best Small Fictions 2016* and cited in the 2016 Pushcart Prize volume, *The Best American Essays 2015*, and *The Best American Travel Writing 2015*. His podcast and writing can be found at www.davidnaimon.com

EXCERPTS